Since You Have Been Raised

Since You Have Been Raised

SERMONS
AND ADDRESSES

Robert A. Hand

Madison House

Published in 2021 by
Madison House
Tyler, TX 75703

Print ISBN: 978-0-5783-0320-8
Ebook ISBN: 978-0-5783-0322-2

Proceeds from sales of this volume benefit Living Water
International (Water.cc) and For the Silent (ForTheSilent.org).

In memoriam
J. I. Packer (1926–2020)

CONTENTS

Preface / vii

PREFACE

I am not a pastor or minster. I am a layperson who tries to do my part when needed, and I occasionally preach and teach as a way to give back to the faith that I have received so much from. These sermons were originally given at three different churches in east Texas between 2018 and 2021. They have been revised and modified for print.

In the spring of 2020, the church we were attending at the time not only closed its doors for months, like so many others, but was also without a pastor. The address "Following Christ in Times of Transition" was a series of reflections delivered to our congregation to address these challenges. The second address, "Biblical Theology and the Christian Life," is a final class lecture I have given to students at LeTourneau University.

Thanks to Jeff Reimer and Bethany Murphy, two of the best editors I know, for their help.

Robert A. Hand
All Saints' Day, 2021

Sermons

NUNC DIMITTIS

The Song of Simeon (Luke 2:22–40)

And when the time came for their purification
according to the Law of Moses, they brought him
up to Jerusalem to present him to the Lord (as it
is written in the Law of the Lord, "Every male who
first opens the womb shall be called holy to the
Lord") and to offer a sacrifice according to what is
said in the Law of the Lord, "a pair of turtledoves,
or two young pigeons." Now there was a man in
Jerusalem, whose name was Simeon, and this
man was righteous and devout, waiting for the
consolation of Israel, and the Holy Spirit was upon
him. And it had been revealed to him by the Holy
Spirit that he would not see death before he had
seen the Lord's Christ. And he came in the Spirit
into the temple, and when the parents brought
in the child Jesus, to do for him according to the

custom of the Law, he took him up in his arms and blessed God and said,

"Lord, now you are letting your servant depart in peace, according to your word; for my eyes have seen your salvation that you have prepared in the presence of all peoples, a light for revelation to the Gentiles, and for glory to your people Israel."

And his father and his mother marveled at what was said about him. And Simeon blessed them and said to Mary his mother, "Behold, this child is appointed for the fall and rising of many in Israel . . . so that thoughts from many hearts may be revealed."

And there was a prophetess, Anna, the daughter of Phanuel, of the tribe of Asher. She was advanced in years, having lived with her husband seven years from when she was a virgin, and then as a widow until she was eighty-four. She did not depart from the temple, worshiping with fasting and prayer night and day. And coming up at that very hour she began to give thanks to God and to speak of him to all who were waiting for the redemption of Jerusalem.

And when they had performed everything according to the Law of the Lord, they returned into Galilee, to their own town of Nazareth. And the child grew and became strong, filled with wisdom. And the favor of God was upon him.

The Sunday after Christmas is one of the most overlooked days in the church calendar. We just finished celebrating the birth of Christ, one of the high points in the Western church year, and after spending many weeks in expectation and anticipation, all is quiet all of a sudden. What now? What comes next? This passage from Luke 2 offers some guidance. The first part of Luke 2 is where we get the traditional Christmas story from—angels, shepherds, wise men, and so forth—but that's just the beginning, and we have a lot of Gospel left to cover. Luke 2:22–40 gets us started on that path.

I often tell students that repetition is one of the first things to look for when reading a passage of Scripture. The authors of the biblical texts we have today did not use bold and italic text for emphasis in the same ways we do today; when they wanted to emphasize something, they repeated it. In the first part of this passage, for example, "the Law of the Lord" is repeated several times, and this gives us a clue for

3

what to focus on in the rest of the passage. Luke's Gospel only uses this term a handful of times, and they are highly concentrated here for some reason. One possibility is that he wants to emphasize how thoroughly Jewish Jesus really was—he was not just of Jewish lineage but had also checked all the right ceremonial boxes and grew out of thoroughly Jewish soil. The references to "the Law of the Lord" in this passage refer specifically to Leviticus 12, where God gives Moses the following guidelines:

> Speak to the people of Israel, saying, "If a woman conceives and bears a male child . . . she shall bring to the priest at the entrance of the tent of meeting a lamb a year old for a burnt offering, and a pigeon or a turtledove for a sin offering, and he shall offer it before the LORD and make atonement for her. . . . *And if she cannot afford a lamb, then she shall take two turtledoves or two pigeons*, one for a burnt offering and the other for a sin offering. And the priest shall make atonement for her, and she shall be clean." (Lev. 12:2–8; emphasis added)

In addition to hearing the consistency with the law, Luke's original hearers would have also been able to read between these lines: Jesus' parents were not people of means.

But why Simeon and Anna? Why are they in the story in the first place? They don't *do* anything, after all. Simeon's declaration beginning in verse 28 has come to be known as the *Nunc dimittis*, and starting as early as the fourth century, it was repeated as a traditional prayer at the end of the day. It also borrows heavily from Isaiah 40–66, which emphasizes the coming messiah, the salvation of all nations. It's a way to tie together what is happening now with this child and what had been foreseen centuries ago.

Some commentators suggest that Simeon's use of the word "now"—*nun* (νύν)—at the beginning of his song appears in a place of emphasis. If this is the case, we could imagine hearing Simeon breathe a loud sigh of relief: "Lord, *now . . . finally!*" Or perhaps less reverently, "It's about time!" The term he uses for "Lord"—*despotēs* (δεσπότης)—is also interesting. It's where we get the English word *despot* from, and I don't think it's the word I would have chosen personally. But it's not an accident that Luke chooses this particular word rather than a more generic term for "Lord" such as *kyrios* (χυριος). It's commonly paired

5

with the word *doulos* (δοῦλος), which means "slave," and it refers specifically to someone who has legal control and authority over someone, as in the case of servants. To add insult to injury, the term he uses for "depart"—*apolyō* (ἀπολύω)—has some very specific connotations. It can refer to granting acquittal or freeing a prisoner, releasing someone from custody, or even dissolving a marriage.

In this particular case, it's best defined as a dismissal, but I think it's important to bear in mind how serious some of the connotations of the term are. I take this to mean that the call to waiting on Christ is anything but casual. I also think Luke's emphasis on Simeon's song suggests that the coming of Christ takes place because of God's initiative in coming to us rather than anything we've done to work our own way to God.

What about Anna? She has impeccable credentials as an Israelite, and she also has impeccable credentials as one who is fully devoted to God. Specifically, for someone in her situation, the ideal spiritual life within Israel was to marry once and then devote one's widowhood to God. And we learn in verse 37 that "*she never left*" the temple in her old age. She doesn't have a song that is equivalent to Simeon's. This doesn't meet our standards of equality at first glance, but commentator Joel Green suggests that "Luke devotes more time to emphasizing Anna's *reliability* than to her *reaction*."[1]

Simeon and Anna *together*, furthermore, give us an even clearer picture of devotion to God; they are more than the sum of their parts. Joel Green continues to note that Simeon and Anna "represent the best of expectant Israel and testify to the central place Jesus already occupies in God's redemptive plan."[2] But Green wasn't the first to note this. Thomas Aquinas actually takes matters a step further and suggests that "[Christ] was made known both to men and to women—namely, to Anna—so as to show no condition of men to be excluded from Christ's redemption."[3] Origen of Alexandria (c. 184–c. 253)

1. Joel B. Green, *The Gospel of Luke*, NICNT (Grand Rapids: Eerdmans, 1997), 150; emphasis added.

2. Green, *Gospel of Luke*, 143.

3. Thomas Aquinas, *Summa theologiae*, trans. Fathers of the English Dominican Province (New York: Benziger Bros., 1947), III.36.3.resp.

likewise notes that it was important for Anna to be included in the story because this was not just another priestly formality; this was an event that cut to the root of life itself, both male and female, as in creation.[4]

It turns out that there is a long tradition of viewing Simeon and Anna as models for us in the life of faith. Saint Augustine observes that Simeon has spent a lifetime patiently waiting on God, and he finally beholds with his eyes what he has only hoped for in faith.[5] This is what we can look forward to as well. Origen focuses on the phrase "he took him up in his arms" and suggests that in similar fashion, we also must embrace Christ in our own arms during our earthly lives, and then we can be dismissed as faithful servants.[6] "Old Simeon and Anna," Karl Barth states, "who waited for the consolation of Israel and

4. Origen of Alexandria, *Homilies on Luke*, trans. Joseph T. Lienhard, Fathers of the Church 94 (Washington, DC: Catholic University of America Press, 1996), 74.

5. Augustine, *Sermon 277*, *Works of Saint Augustine* III/8 (Hyde Park, NY: New City Press, 1994), 44.

6. Origen, *Homilies on Luke*, 74.

the deliverance of Jerusalem, are now dismissed like faithful sentinels whose duty is done."[7]

For my own part, I think Simeon and Anna teach us that in the life of faith, hopefulness, patience, attention, and receptivity can be more important than performance, accomplishments, and striving. While progress and success in our professional lives depends on how much effort we put forth, how clever we are, how hard we work, what connections we make, and so on, in the life of Christian faith, this doesn't work very well. In fact, I would argue that "success" and "progress" aren't even the right categories. In this sense, neither Simeon nor Anna is a model of success. In fact, they are failures. They don't produce anything, they don't sell anything, they don't contribute anything—they just wait and hope. *And yet*, they are the ones who were attentive to the Spirit and recognized what was really going on.

Luke suggests to us that their apprehension of the miracle of the birth of Christ was related to their

7. Karl Barth, *Church Dogmatics*, ed. and trans. Geoffrey Bromiley and T. F. Torrance (Edinburgh: T&T Clark, 1977), V/2, 34.

lack of credentials, not because they were accomplished individuals. Put differently, they don't *do* anything . . . and that's exactly the point. Hoping, waiting, expecting, and "paying attention" are central to the life of Christian faith. Simone Weil states, "We do not obtain the most precious gifts by going in search of them but by waiting for them. Man cannot discover them by his own powers, and if he sets out to seek for them he will find in their place counterfeits of which he will be unable to discern their falsity."[8]

As we consider Simeon and Anna—quiet and unassuming figures during a quiet and unassuming moment in the church year—maybe we can resolve to likewise simply be attentive to what God has done, is doing in our midst, and promises to do in Christ. We can also take a look back and be hopeful, grateful, and joyful because God has come to us in Jesus Christ, not because of anything we've done, but because it is in his nature to not leave us alone. All the information we need as followers of Christ has already been

8. Simone Weil, *Waiting for God* (New York: Harper, 2009), 62.

revealed once and for all to Simeon and Anna. There is no additional information left to be disclosed, and now, finally, we can also go in peace.

2

DOES CHURCH MATTER?

Paul and Catholicity (Rom. 15:24–29)

In recent weeks we've been exploring the question, "Why church?" Do I really need to go to church? Can't I just be spiritual and not religious? We've been using the Nicene Creed as a guide to answering these questions: "We believe . . . in one holy catholic and apostolic church." When we recite these words, we are joining with Christians not just across place but also across time—Christians have been reciting these words for nearly two thousand years. I'm going to focus on the term "catholic," which comes from the Greek word *katholikos* (καθολικός), simply meaning "general or universal." We get the term by combining the words *kata* and *holos*, which literally means "according to the whole." I need to acknowledge that there is great disagreement about this term. There is the Roman Catholic Church with a capital "C," but that's not what I'll be referring to. I'll be using the term *catholic* in a general sense, with a lowercase "c": the communion of saints across all times and places, regardless of denomination.

The exact term *catholic* does not appear in Scripture, but although it's not necessarily there by name, it is absolutely there in spirit. Paul had great concern for Christians across the Mediterranean. Consider this passage from Romans 15:

> I hope to see you in passing as I go to Spain, and to be helped on my journey there by you, once I have enjoyed your company for a while. At present, however, I am going to Jerusalem bringing aid to the saints. For Macedonia and Achaia have been pleased to make some contribution for the poor among the saints at Jerusalem. For they were pleased to do it, and indeed they owe it to them. For if the Gentiles have come to share in their spiritual blessings, they ought also to be of service to them in material blessings. When therefore I have completed this and have delivered to them what has been collected, I will leave for Spain by way of you. I know that when I come to you I

will come in the fullness of the blessing of Christ.
(Rom. 15:24–29)

It turns out that this collection was one of the major concerns of Paul's missionary career. And it wasn't just a nice gesture; Paul's beliefs about Jesus Christ's resurrection and ascension have profound consequences not just for how he lives personally but how the "catholic," or whole, church all over his world holds together and looks after each other. He refers to it again in 1 Corinthians 16:

> Now concerning the collection for the saints: as I directed the churches of Galatia, so you also are to do. On the first day of every week, each of you is to put something aside and store it up, as he may prosper, so that there will be no collecting when I come. And when I arrive, I will send those whom you accredit by letter to carry your gift to Jerusalem. If it seems advisable that I should go also, they will accompany me. (1 Cor. 16:1–4)

Rome, Corinth, Galatia, Jerusalem, Macedonia (Thessalonica) . . . this collection was a visible and tangible way to unite the scattered bodies of Christ. It was a consequence of his beliefs about the resurrected and ascended Christ. Commentator Raymond Brown notes, "Both psychologically and practically there are few things in life that bind together people and institutions more effectively than sharing their bank accounts."[1]

But the question remains: *Why?* Why wasn't just *believing* in Jesus good enough? Why go out of his way to unite the churches across the Mediterranean in this way? Why not just stay home with a cup of coffee and watch church online? Here's one clue: when God deals with people in Scripture, it is often with groups of people, not individuals. When God does deal with individuals, one of two things is typically true: (1) they're in trouble, or (2) they're being called for some special purpose so that they can go back to the people and speak or act on God's behalf. Consider Jeremiah 29:11–13, for instance: "For I know the plans I have for you, declares the LORD, plans for welfare and not for evil, to give you a future and a hope. Then you will call upon me and come

1. Raymond Brown, *An Introduction to the New Testament* (New Haven: Yale University Press, 1977), 553.

and pray to me, and I will hear you. You will seek me and find me, when you seek me with all your heart." All of the second-person pronouns in this passage are plural, not singular. In 1 Corinthians 3, Paul says, "For we are God's fellow workers. You are God's field, God's building. . . . Do you not know that you are God's temple and that God's Spirit dwells in you? . . . For God's temple is holy, and you are that temple" (1 Cor. 3:9, 16–17). Again, every "you" in this passage is plural. And let's not forget that the Lord's Prayer itself contains no reference to "I" or "me" but rather "we," "our," and "us."

This was *extremely* important in the early church, so much so that being in unity with the catholic/ whole church was a necessary precondition for being a Christian in the first place. The first known use of the word *catholic* comes from Ignatius of Antioch (c. AD 35–c. 107): "Wherever Jesus Christ is, there is the catholic church."[2] Cyprian of Carthage (c. AD 200–258) states more strongly, "Whoever is separated

---

2. Ignatius of Antioch, *Epistle to the Smyrneans*, ANF 1 (Edinburgh: T&T Clark, 1885), chap. 8.

from the Church . . . is separated from the promises of the Church; *nor can he who forsakes the Church of Christ attain to the rewards of Christ. . . . He can no longer have God for his Father, who has not the Church for his mother.*"[3] Closer to our own time, Dietrich Bonhoeffer emphasizes in *Life Together* that visible, united fellowship with other Christians is a gift that God gives to us for our benefit. In theory, God could have left us alone with only abstract truths to guide us through life. But instead God gives us the gift of other people for actual, tangible, visible reassurance of his goodness toward us and for our encouragement and growth in the faith. He states, "The life or death of a Christian community is determined by whether it achieves sober wisdom . . . as soon as possible . . . [in understanding] itself as being a part of the one, holy, catholic Christian Church, where

3. Cyprian of Carthage, "On the Unity of the Church," in *Ante-Nicene Fathers* 5, ed. Alexander Roberts, James Donaldson, and A. Cleveland Coxe, trans. Robert Ernest Wallis (Buffalo, NY: Christian Literature, 1886), 1.6; emphasis added.

it shares actively and passively in the sufferings and struggles and promise of the whole Church."[4]

So, why church? First, I want to suggest that Christian community is an "essential property" of the Christian faith. In order to move into maturity as a follower of Christ, I need to be connected to a larger body. This is particularly challenging for us in North America in the twenty-first century because almost everything in our lives is designed to cater to our individual wants, needs, and wishes. Second, if my faith does not involve other people, it is not going to be as healthy as it could be. We often hear people refer to their "personal relationship with Jesus," which is not a bad thing, but it's also not something you'll find in Scripture. Finally, Christian community is a gift from God to us. It offers encouragement and reassurance.

I mentioned at the beginning that we have been asking the question of whether church really matters. Do I have to go to church? I actually think these are the wrong questions. This is much like receiving a gift

4. Dietrich Bonhoeffer, *Life Together*, trans. John Doberstein (San Francisco: HarperSanFrancisco, 1954), 37.

and asking if you really have to open it. Of course you don't have to open it, but why wouldn't you? We don't *have* to go to church. We *get* to—not because we must, but because we may.

3

THE SPIRIT OF THE LAW

Whitsunday (John 14:15–27)

"If you love me, you will keep my commandments. And I will ask the Father, and he will give you another Helper, to be with you forever, even the Spirit of truth, whom the world cannot receive, because it neither sees him nor knows him. You know him, for he dwells with you and will be in you.

"I will not leave you as orphans; I will come to you. Yet a little while and the world will see me no more, but you will see me. Because I live, you also will live. In that day you will know that I am in my Father, and you in me, and I in you. Whoever has my commandments and keeps them, he it is who loves me. And he who loves me will be loved by my Father, and I will love him and manifest myself to him." Judas (not Iscariot) said to him,

"Lord, how is it that you will manifest yourself to us, and not to the world?" Jesus answered him, "If anyone loves me, he will keep my word, and my Father will love him, and we will come to him and make our home with him. Whoever does not love me does not keep my words. And the word that you hear is not mine but the Father's who sent me.

"These things I have spoken to you while I am still with you. But the Helper, the Holy Spirit, whom the Father will send in my name, he will teach you all things and bring to your remembrance all that I have said to you. Peace I leave with you; my peace I give to you. Not as the world gives do I give to you. Let not your hearts be troubled, neither let them be afraid."

John's Gospel is very different from Matthew's, Mark's, and Luke's. It was written later, to a different audience, under a different set of circumstances. John was likely writing in an environment that was more hostile to followers of Christ; things were more uncertain for them than for the original hearers of Matthew, Mark, and Luke. His audience likely also included more Greeks, so it would make sense for him to use concepts that they were familiar with. John often uses different language and themes to communicate his message: light and darkness, Father and Son, the world and eternal life. We can definitely hear some of this in the reading for today. This passage is part of the "Farewell Discourse," where Jesus is describing to the disciples that he will be leaving soon. Imagine their incredulity: they have accepted his call to follow him, they have heard his claims about himself, they have encountered opposition . . . and now he's leaving?

We'll return to this question, but for now I want to point out the importance of keeping Christ's commandments in this passage. Jesus says, "If you love me, you will keep my commandments" (v. 15); "whoever has my commandments and keeps them, he it is who loves me" (v. 21); "whoever does not love me does not keep my words" (v. 24). Here is what I hear Jesus saying: loving Christ requires action. On one level, this is a classic distinction between word and deed, theory and practice. If you say you are something, that usually entails actions of some kind. I like to think of myself as a good friend, for example, but

I don't always make the efforts I should to maintain friendships. I like to think of myself as a good caretaker of my property, but I have several patches of dead grass right in the front of my yard. I called myself a football player in high school, but I spent a lot of time on the bench. Jesus is saying, If you love me, do what I say.

Jesus tells us what his commandment is in no uncertain terms in the next chapter: "This is my commandment, that you love one another as I have loved you. Greater love has no one than this, that someone lay down his life for his friends. You are my friends if you do what I command you" (John 15:12–14). Another way to put this is that it is one thing to assent to the notion that "loving God" in the abstract sense is a good thing; it is another thing entirely to act on that belief. Hear how fifth-century church father Cyril of Alexandria (c. AD 376–444) puts it:

> Even if a person says that he loves God, he will not immediately merit credit for having true love of God, since the power of virtue does not stand on bare speech alone, nor piety on naked words. Rather, it is distinguished by performance of good deeds and an obedient disposition. *Keeping*

the divine commandments is the best way to give liv-
ing expression to our love toward God. It presents
the picture of a life lived in all its fullness and truth.
It is not a life sketched out in mere sounds that
flow from the tongue. It gleams instead with the
altogether radiant and brilliant colors that paint a
portrait of good works.[1]

I want to acknowledge that we're walking a fine
line here, however, because we're talking about *good
works*, and Protestants don't believe that good works
have anything to do with God's grace, right? Not so
fast. Martin Luther had this to say, and recall that
most Christians in his time did not have access to
written copies of Scripture or were illiterate: "The
Ten Commandments, the Creed, and the Lord's
Prayer . . . contain fully and completely everything
that is in the Scriptures, everything that should ever
be preached, and everything that a Christian needs
to know, put so plainly and briefly that no one can

---

1. Cyril of Alexandria, *Commentary on the Gospel According
to St. John,* trans. T. Randell, Library of Fathers of the Holy
Catholic Church 48 (Oxford: John Henry Parker, 1885), 298–
99; emphasis added.

make complaint or excuse."[2] John Calvin suggested that the law is a guide for how to respond in gratitude to God's grace.[3]

It is true that there is nothing we can do to earn God's grace; it is not true that we can do whatever we want. Following Christ has consequences for how we prioritize and order our lives. Craig Keener states, "Love is not a mere sentiment but defined by specific content through God's commandments."[4] Loving Christ is more than just an idea.

I mentioned earlier that Jesus has called the disciples to follow him, and now he's breaking the news that he's going to leave. The disciples must have been perplexed to say the least. Jesus has this to say in response: "I will ask the Father, and he will give

2. Martin Luther, "A Brief Form of the Ten Commandments, a Brief Form of the Creed, and a Brief Form of the Lord's Prayer (1520)," *Works of Martin Luther* 2 (Philadelphia: Holman, 1915), 354.

3. John Calvin, *Institutes of the Christian Religion*, ed. John T. McNeill, trans. Ford Lewis Battles (Philadelphia: Westminster, 1960), 2.8.

4. Craig Keener, *The Gospel of John: A Commentary*, 2 vols. (Grand Rapids: Baker Academic, 2003), 952.

you another Helper, to be with you forever, even the Spirit of truth, whom the world cannot receive, because it neither sees him nor knows him. You know him, for he dwells with you and will be in you. Yet a little while and the world will see me no more, but you will see me. Because I live, you also will live. In that day you will know that I am in my Father, and you in me, and I in you."

It's worth noting that passages like this are where the doctrine of the Trinity comes from. But I'd like to focus on some of the ways the Spirit is described in this passage. First, the Spirit is referred to as "another" helper. The church fathers placed great significance on this one word. It suggests that Jesus himself was a comforter of some sort, and Gregory Nazianzus (AD 329–390) suggested that John inserted this word "so that you might acknowledge his co-equality."[5] Second, the term used for "helper" is *parakletos* (παράκλετος), which is a term used for a legal advocate. It is the opposite of *katēgōros* (κατήγωρος),

5. Gregory Nazianzus, *Oration 41: On Pentecost*, NPNF[2] 7 (Edinburgh: T&T Clark, 1952), 383.

which means "accuser." (John's Gospel is full of legal and trial imagery.) Finally, Jesus refers to the Spirit of "truth." This is good news for the disciples because wherever and however the Spirit guides them will be entirely consistent with what Christ has taught them. Karl Barth states, "The Spirit is 'the Spirit of truth,' the power that does not work arbitrarily or independently, but simply declares Jesus, accomplishing again and again the disclosure and revelation of his reality."[6]

I mentioned earlier that it was important not just to love God in the abstract—not just to assent to the idea of loving God—but to actually do it. In the giving of the Spirit, *this is exactly what God does for us.* God does not just love *us* in the abstract but actually gives us what we need to understand God and love God and one another. I've said that love of God requires action. But notice the particular way Christ describes it here: it is surrounded by language of reassurance, love, and affection. *Christ did not say, "I*

6. Karl Barth, *Church Dogmatics*, trans. Geoffrey Bromiley and T. F. Torrance (Edinburgh: T&T Clark, 1977), V/2, 163.

demand you to follow these rules or else." He establishes the context of divine love first, then reminds them that this entails certain behavior, and then *reassures them* his Spirit will always be with them to help guide them.

Recall that the disciples in this passage were likely confused and afraid of the fact that Christ was leaving them. Let me pose this question for us: Have you ever felt like God has left you? Christ is telling us in this passage that he hasn't. Do you currently feel as though God is absent? Christ is telling us in this passage that he isn't. If and when God feels distant, know that he is near. Know also that the Christian life requires effort. If I say I love God, I need to do what God says. Sometimes if God feels distant or we are disoriented in our faith, what we really need to do is get to work. But not the sort of effort and labor that seeks to *earn* the grace of God; that is already given to us freely. Rather it's the sort of effort that seeks to actively draw near to God, who has already drawn near to us, in gratitude and thanksgiving, and then to extend that same grace to other people.

You will experience times in your faith when you feel reassured, and times when you feel without hope.

Christ is telling us in this passage that the Spirit that God gives to us is one of remembrance, reassurance, and hope. So be reassured, and hear one last time what our Lord Jesus Christ is saying to us all: "The Helper, the Holy Spirit, whom the Father will send in my name, he will teach you all things and bring to your remembrance all that I have said to you. Peace I leave with you; my peace I give to you. Not as the world gives do I give to you. Let not your hearts be troubled, neither let them be afraid."

4

SINCE YOU HAVE BEEN RAISED

Life After Pentecost (Col. 3:1–11)

[Since] you have been raised with Christ, seek the things that are above, where Christ is, seated at the right hand of God. Set your minds on things that are above, not on things that are on earth. For you have died, and your life is hidden with Christ in God. When Christ who is your life appears, then you also will appear with him in glory.

Put to death therefore what is earthly in you: sexual immorality, impurity, passion, evil desire, and covetousness, which is idolatry. On account of these the wrath of God is coming. In these you too once walked, when you were living in them. But now you must put them all away: anger, wrath, malice, slander, and obscene talk from your mouth. Do not lie to one another, seeing that you have put off the old self with its practices and

have put on the new self, which is being renewed
in knowledge after the image of its creator. Here
there is not Greek and Jew, circumcised and
uncircumcised, barbarian, Scythian, slave, free;
but Christ is all, and in all.

It's important to remember that the New Testament
letters are personal correspondence that we get to listen in on. They are not formal doctrinal pronounce-
ments. Rather we are walking in on conversations
that are already underway. What was the situation
in Colossae in this case? It was one of three cities
in a forgotten part of the Roman Empire: Laodecia,
Hierapolis, and Colossae. Among those three, it was
the least significant. However, in past centuries, it
was a highly celebrated city. So we have a group of
people in a small town who were likely living in the
shadow of better days. Surely some of us can relate
to that.

The beginning of Colossians details who Christ is;
now, mid-way through chapter 2, Paul starts to get
into what that might mean for his readers. You'll notice strong contrasts between things like heaven and

earth, above and below, earthly and spiritual, visibility and hiddenness in this part of the letter. What I'd like to do is work through this passage and point out what I think are some of the most important themes.

First, this passage reminds us that the Christian life is a *spiritual* life. This is an unpopular opinion of sorts because we love all things holistic and embodied. But there is an undeniably spiritual, that is, metaphysical, dimension to who we are as human beings; we are more than the sum of our parts. This is important to keep in mind as we proceed, because on the ground in Colossae during this time, strange philosophies were circulating. No one is really sure where they originated from exactly or what they entailed, but one of Paul's motives in the letter is to respond to these philosophies. In order to do so, it is significant that Paul opens this chapter not by saying something like, "Because we believe in this alternative philosophy . . ." Rather he says, "*Since you have been raised* . . ." Paul also does not say something along the lines of, "Because God is vengeful and angry, do what you're told." Rather "*Since you have been raised*, set your mind on things above." Issac of Nineveh (c. 613–c. 700), an ancient Syrian Christian from the area currently known as Bahrain and Qatar, suggested that being raised with Christ is an exodus from our captivity to darkness.[1] It's not just a belief; it's a reality. (As a side note, students of Greek will also recall how indicative statements give way to imperative statements: "*x* is the case, therefore go and do *y* and *z*.") Second, Paul suggests that "since you have been raised . . . *put to death* therefore all that is earthly in you." The term translated "put to death" is *nekrō-sate* (νεκρώσατε), which comes from the same root as the word for "corpse." This is unusually strong language; it could also be translated as "slaughter," "take no prisoners," or "have no mercy." John Chrysostom (c. 347–c. 407), an ancient Christian who served as bishop of Constantinople, likened this command to scouring rust off a statue and also taking any measures necessary to prevent future rust.[2]

Note also that this passage contains both active and passive injunctions. There is a certain division of

1. Isaac of Nineveh, *Aescetical Homilies*, ed. Dana Miller (Boston: Holy Transfiguration Monastery, 1984), 175.
2. John Chrysostom, *Homilies on Colossians*, NPNF[1] 13 (Edinburgh: T&T Clark, 1889), 294.

labor in the spiritual life; God has raised us (passive), but we also have work to do (active). A good portion of the work Paul indicates we need to do in light of being raised in Christ is to "put to death" such things as "sexual immorality, impurity, passion, evil desire, and covetousness." Ancient philosophy and the church fathers referred to such things as "the passions," and they are full of wisdom on this subject. "The passions" can be summarized as irrational motives and desires that lead to wrongful conduct. Paul lists a handful of specific vices, *but they all start with being passionate about the wrong things*, and the root of them all is love of self. Maximus the Confessor (c. 580–662), an ancient Christian theologian from the modern-day country known as Georgia, bordered by Russia to the north and Turkey to the south, went so far as to say that we should conduct *warfare* on our bodily passions. The way to do this, Maximus suggested, was to first "remove the effect of sin, then backtrack to its cause."[3] We could liken this to gardening: it requires

3. Maximus Confessor, "Four Hundred Chapters on Love," in *Maximus Confessor: Selected Writings*, trans. George Berthold (Mahwah, NJ: Paulist Press, 1985), 1.84.

constant, vigilant, active attention. Gardens must be weeded, treated for insects, and protected. This passage, I think, is saying something similar: uproot the weeds so that Christian virtues can grow.

The last thing I'd like to point out is the phrase "here there is not Greek and Jew . . ." It is interesting to me that Paul waits until the very end of this passage to mention identity categories. Compare this to our culture's current obsession with all things related to identity: gender, race, class, and so on. This passage suggests that "since you have been raised," these things are much less relevant than we are led to believe. Commentator F. F. Bruce even goes so far as to say, "Within the community of the new creation—'in Christ'—these barriers were *irrelevant*; indeed, they had no existence. . . . Where cultural differences exist, the gospel ignores them."[4]

We have been raised up in Christ, so let's set our minds on *that* fact, not on arbitrary cultural and sociological categories. Once we have our minds

---

4. F. F. Bruce, *The Epistles to the Colossians, to Philemon, and to the Ephesians*, NICNT (Grand Rapids: Eerdmans, 1984), 177–78; emphasis added.

pointed in this direction, we can appreciate the division of labor in the spiritual life: God has done some things in Christ, and we are responsible for doing our part. *We have been raised up* in Christ, and where we choose to focus our effort and energy is up to us. This passage encourages us to redirect our attention to things above and get to work on ourselves in light of that reassuring fact and the confidence it provides.

5

THE GOOD NEWS OF THE LAW

Galatians 3:23–25; 4:4–7

Now before faith came, we were held captive under the law, imprisoned until the coming faith would be revealed. So then, the law was our guardian until Christ came, in order that we might be justified by faith. But now that faith has come, we are no longer under a guardian, for in Christ Jesus you are all sons of God, through faith. . . . But when the fullness of time had come, God sent forth his Son, born of woman, born under the law, to redeem those who were under the law, so that we might receive adoption as sons. And because you are sons, God has sent the Spirit of his Son into our hearts, crying, "Abba! Father!" So you are no longer a slave, but a son, and if a son, then an heir through God.

We've spent several weeks looking forward in antici-pation to the birth of Christ. The time has come and gone, and now we face an important question: *Now what?* Or maybe for some of us, the question is really, *So what?* I'd like to try to answer those questions this morning by reflecting on what Paul has to say to us through two passages: Galatians 3:23–26 and 4:4–7.

Our text for today is a good summary of one of *the* central challenges of our faith: the relationship between the good news of the gospel of Jesus Christ and the law. The good news of the gospel is that God has freely done in Christ what we couldn't do for our-selves. The law, at least as it was given to Israel, makes demands of us and our behavior. At first glance, Paul seems to be saying that the law is no longer relevant for us today now that Christ has come. But is this really what he's saying?

Galatians was written sometime between AD 48 and 57 either to Christians in a particular geograph-ical location *or* to the ethnic group of Galatians. Either way, they were mostly Gentiles, that is, non-Jews. The specific issue in Galatia was that Christians in Galatia started entertaining "other gospels" after Paul left. They started adding legal requirements to the gospel; in other words, they took a step backward! Paul's response to them is not only that no one is justified by the law, but also that *no one ever was* justified by the law—even in the Old Testament. To support this argument, Paul uses the example of Abraham. "Know then that it is those of faith who are the sons of Abraham. And the Scripture, foreseeing that God would justify the Gentiles by faith, preached the gospel beforehand to Abraham, saying, 'In you shall all the nations be blessed.' So then, those who are of faith are blessed along with Abraham, the man of faith" (3:7–9). He also asks the rhetorical question, "Is the law then contrary to the promises of God? Certainly not! For *if a law had been given that could give life, then righteousness would indeed be by the law*" (3:21; emphasis added).

We often assume that the Old Testament is all about law, and the New Testament is all about grace. But according to Paul, all of Scripture, from start to finish, is about grace. In the beginning, God didn't make legal demands; in the beginning, God created the heavens and the earth and male and female in his image, and it was very good. In the beginning wasn't chaos and disorder and violence; in the beginning was the Word, and the Word was with God, and the Word was God. The people of Israel cried out to God in their slavery, and God didn't say, "Do what I say, and then I will bless you"; God heard them, God saw them, God remembered his promises, and God rescued them from their slavery in Egypt. In the wilderness God gives Israel the Ten Commandments, what we know as the law, but note that the law doesn't appear until after God has established a long history of keeping his promises to his people.

In Deuteronomy, the law is described in this way:

> Fear the LORD your God . . . by keeping all his statutes and his commandments . . . all the days of your life . . . that your days may be long. Hear therefore, O Israel, and be careful to do them, *that it may go well with you*, and that you may multiply greatly. (Deut. 6:2–3; emphasis added)

> When your son asks you in time to come, "What is the meaning of the testimonies and the statutes and the rules that the LORD our God has commanded you?" then you shall say to your son, *"We were Pharaoh's slaves in Egypt. And the LORD*

brought us out of Egypt with a mighty hand." (Deut. 6:20–21; emphasis added)

All throughout Scripture, we see the following pattern. First, God takes the initiative to create or save his people or keep his promises. Then and only then, God gives his people guidelines for how to live *so that things will go well for them.* Christ has come among us in a way that is entirely consistent with how God has been acting all along: for our sake and for our salvation. It is with this in mind that Paul says that the law was our guardian until Christ came. It wasn't intended to provide a way *to* God but rather a way for God to preserve his people.

A few textual notes. Paul uses an interesting term for the law here: *paidagōgon* (παιδαγωγόν). This term literally means "boy leader": in the Greco-Roman Empire, it was a slave who escorted freeborn youth to and from school. Another interesting phrase is "But when the fullness of time had come." Another translation renders this as "when the term was complete." I sense that Paul is suggesting something like the end of a gestation period; God's promises have been gestating for years, and in the coming of Christ, they came to full term. I'd also like to emphasize two inconspicuous words in this passage, both of them prepositions: "*under*" and "*in.*" "We are no longer under a guardian," Paul states, "for *in* Christ Jesus you are all sons of God, through faith" (Gal. 3:25–26). The law was something we lived *under* until the fullness of time had come, but now we are *in* Christ. We have arrived.

Let me suggest an analogy for this. Our daughters, like most kids, love their phones. In an effort to help them navigate today's digital world, we give them a contract when they receive the gift of their first phone. The contract is actually for their own benefit. We have long since established our unconditional love toward them, and the contract is an extension of that. They don't earn our love by observing the contract. The goal for them "in the fullness of time" is for them to not even need a contract at all.

Faith in Christ works in much the same way. You cannot do anything to earn God's favor; it has already been given. God has taken the initiative to do what is best for us as his adopted children.

I recognize that we all come to these matters from different places. Let me mention a few possible scenarios. First, maybe you find yourself anxious about never living up to God's expectations. I have good news for you: you're actually right, and you're closer to the gospel than you might think!

Second, maybe you find yourself thinking that the way you behave and the choices you make are inconsequential because you are saved by grace. I have good news and bad news for you: you're off on the right foot, but your choices actually do have consequences.

Third, maybe you find yourself looking down on other people because you've got everything together and no one else does. Bad news: you've missed the point. Jesus didn't come to enforce the law but to fulfill it through self-sacrificial love.

At the beginning of the sermon I mentioned that the question we face now after Christmas is "Now what?" Let me offer some New Year's resolutions for each scenario. If you find yourself holding others to standards they can't possibly meet, remember that we are all adopted children and did not earn our place in God's household. Try taking one step closer toward the people you dislike and get to know them.

If you find yourself spiritually lazy because God has done all the work for you, it might be time to wake up. Christ is coming back, and the Scriptures teach that we will give an account not just of what we've done but also of what we've failed to do.

If you find yourself anxious about pleasing God, you are in good company. The Gospels are full of people who come to Jesus in their times of need, and he always welcomes them. Open your heart in gratitude to what God has done for you. And for all of us, bear in mind in this new year that we are no longer slaves but children and even heirs *in*, not *under*, Jesus Christ our Lord.

6

LAST WORDS OF CHRIST

"You Will Be with Me in Paradise" (Luke 23:32–43)

Two others, who were criminals, were led away to be put to death with him. And when they came to the place that is called The Skull, there they crucified him, and the criminals, one on his right and one on his left. And Jesus said, "Father, forgive them, for they know not what they do." And they cast lots to divide his garments. And the people stood by, watching, but the rulers scoffed at him, saying, "He saved others; let him save himself, if he is the Christ of God, his Chosen One!" The soldiers also mocked him, coming up and offering him sour wine and saying, "If you are the King of the Jews, save yourself!" There was also an inscription over him, "This is the King of the Jews."

One of the criminals who were hanged railed at him, saying, "Are you not the Christ? Save yourself and us!" But the other rebuked him, saying, "Do you not fear God, since you are under the same sentence of condemnation? And we indeed justly, for we are receiving the due reward of our deeds; but this man has done nothing wrong." And he said, "Jesus, remember me when you come into your kingdom." And he said to him, "Truly, I say to you, today you will be with me in paradise."

In recent weeks we have been meditating on Jesus' last words. Last week, we discussed Jesus' prayer, "Forgive them, for they know not what they do." I'd actually like to pick up here briefly because a couple of other things have occurred to me since then. There is a precedent in Jewish tradition to plead for vengeance. Second Chronicles records the following regarding Joash's son: "And when he was dying, he said, 'May the Lord see and avenge!' (2 Chron. 24:22). Psalm 137 states, "Babylon . . . blessed shall he be who repays you with what you have done to us!" (v. 8). In Jeremiah 15, we read, "O Lord, remember me and visit me, and take vengeance for me on my persecutors" (Jer. 15:15). With this is mind, Jesus had every right to cry out in anger for justice to be done, for retribution. Instead he says, in effect, "Forgive them, be patient with them; they just don't see it. They don't know what they're doing."

Another custom in Jewish tradition was that if you falsely accuse someone of a crime—which is what is being done to Jesus in this story—and it is found out after the fact that your case is fraudulent, you become responsible for bearing the penalty of the alleged crime. In this case, Jesus' Jewish accusers are running the risk of being put to death themselves if they are wrong. Jesus knows this, and could have easily said, "I will be vindicated! As it has been done to me, let it be done to you." Instead he expresses patience and compassion.

Let this serve as an entry point into today's text. By way of reminder, we are approaching one of the central mysteries of our faith. Jesus has spent his life making some grand claims about his authority. Now he is being executed like a common criminal. All indications are that he has failed. As we consider this mystery, join me in working our way gradually from the outside of the scene in toward the two thieves on the crosses next to Jesus. Pay close attention to the other characters and what they're doing, and listen for how the action intensifies as we draw closer. The people . . . stood by. The rulers . . . scoffed. The soldiers . . . mocked. The responses to Jesus escalate quickly from idly standing by to actively mocking him. "If you are the king of the Jews, save yourself!" they taunt (v. 37). This is similar to Jesus' temptation in the wilderness in Luke 4: "If you are the Son of God, tell this stone to become bread . . . throw yourself down from here" (vv. 3, 9).

As we move closer to Jesus and the two criminals, we see the language intensify even more. The people stood by, the rulers scoffed, the soldiers mocked, but then we read that "one of the criminals *railed*, 'Are you not the Christ? Save yourself and save us!'" The word translated as "railed" is *eblasphēmei* (ἐβλασφήμει). He literally *blasphemed* Jesus; he *verbally abused him*. He *reviled* him.

But the other criminal *rebuked* the first one for his verbal abuse. There is a long tradition of reading these two criminals as examples of how we tend to respond to Christ; the two criminals in a way "prefigure" two ways people would come to respond to Jesus. The second criminal's rebuke is an interesting and powerful statement: he indicates that he clearly separates himself from the first criminal from the outset. We might say, "The other strongly disagreed, and indicted him," as in a court of law. This repentant thief has come to be known in the Christian tradition as "Saint Dismas." Interestingly, the town of San Dimas, California, is named after him, as well as the Church of the Good Thief in Kingston, Ontario, which was built by the residents of the nearby correctional facility. He is also commemorated in a traditional Eastern Orthodox prayer that is said before receiving the Eucharist: "I will not speak of Thy Mystery to Thine enemies, neither like Judas will I give Thee a kiss; but like the thief will I confess Thee: Remember me, O Lord in Thy Kingdom."

Notice how different what he says to Jesus is from the other criminal. He doesn't say to Jesus, "Prove yourself," but rather, "Remember me." "I recognize that the fault is not with you, God," he seems to say, "but rather with me." Jesus' response to him seems to indicate, "You get it. I recognize that you understand what is realliy going on here, and today you will be with me in paradise."

Do you remember another reference to paradise early on in the Bible? The last time we read about entering or exiting paradise, Adam and Eve were being sent out. There is also a long interpretive tradition that attaches great significance to this moment not just because it is profound in its own right but because it connects the entire biblical story together. In Genesis, the first humans are sent out of paradise. Now, through Christ, the gates are open to the humble. One Eastern Orthodox prayer states, "Eden's locked gates the Thief has opened wide, by putting in the key, 'Remember me.'"

The question that stands before us all is, Where am I in this story? Where am I this season of Lent, as we are confronted with the mystery of the crucifixion of the Son of God? Let's start on the outside and work our way back in. Maybe you're indifferent this season. Maybe you're one of the people who stood by, watching. Maybe you're a step closer than that. Maybe you come to this season with your act completely together, and this whole thing is kind of a waste of time. Maybe you come to this season and you think you understand it all, and you're scoffing, thinking, *This is all kind of ridiculous.*

Maybe you're even a step closer than that. You're actually seeing all this close up, and it just doesn't make sense. A king who is weak? Are you kidding me? If this is you—if you're on the outside and indifferent to this whole thing or maybe even find yourself mocking it—my encouragement to you is this: take one step closer, and listen to what Christ has to say.

As we move closer to the crucified Christ, we find something interesting. Our responses are often not one of just a simple acceptance or rejection. One criminal doesn't just reject Jesus; he demands Jesus to act on his behalf: "God, I demand that you go out of your way to fix this mess in *my* world, *my* kingdom." The other doesn't just casually accept Jesus; the other one admits that he's in over his head, gives thanks to God, and humbly prays, "Remember me when you come into *your* kingdom."

We often are either outright angry with God, or we are broken and humble. Jesus' response to the outsiders, rulers, soldiers, and even the angry criminal is silence. To the criminal who humbles himself before the mystery of the crucified Christ, his response is, "I am with you, and you will be with me." What we don't hear are words of anger, judgment, or revenge.

I wonder what difficulties you have faced in the past. How about currently? Do you feel like you are enduring unnecessary, disorienting difficulty? Have you ever felt angry at God? There are two ways of responding. We could ask, "Where are you, God? I have done nothing wrong. My circumstances are unjust. I don't deserve this." Another option is, "God I don't understand what is happening, but I trust in your goodness. Please don't forget about me."

We can't always understand why our circumstances are the way they are, but we can choose how we respond. We can stand by and watch; we can scoff; we can ridicule; we can even blaspheme. Christ is present, and he is patient. He might be silent, but he is there. If you find yourself railing at God, hear this: God is right next you, suffering with you. The option other than anger is actually not as dramatic as you might think. It's not enthusiasm, celebration, or conversion. It's humility: Lord I believe, help my unbelief. Don't forget about me. And that's all Christ asks.

7

THE WISDOM OF CHRIST

Understanding the Book of Proverbs

A couple of weeks ago we dove right into the book of Proverbs. We're about halfway through, and we thought it might be good to devote a Sunday to asking some big-picture questions, like, What exactly *is* the book of Proverbs? Where did it come from? Who wrote it? Why do we have it in the first place? Where does this piece fit in the big puzzle of Scripture? What are some of the main themes? We'll start with the big picture, then consider some background information about how the book fits together as a whole. I'll close with some comments about Proverbs and how it connects to Jesus.

One of my objectives whenever I teach Scripture is to demonstrate that Scripture is one, cohesive, connected book. It's not just a random collection of information. It has a lot of moving parts, but in God's providence, they all fit together. Proverbs belongs to what's known as wisdom literature, which includes Psalms, Job, Ecclesiastes, Lamentations, and Song of Songs. What all these books have in common is, first of all, they are all in the Old Testament. They also take a break from the history of Israel and address more universal themes. Most of the Old Testament is narrative and stories—creation, exodus, the law; the historical books; the prophets who are trying to get God's people back on track. With wisdom literature, we get inside the heads of some of the characters. You might say they deal with issues related to "real life": disappointment, joy, relationships, anger, intimacy, money.

Israel wasn't the only ancient culture that had collections of proverbs—this was a common thing to have. Ancient Egypt, ancient China, India— they all have their collections of proverbial wisdom. Interestingly, most ancient Middle Eastern wisdom literature was reserved for the training of the nobility for their duties in royal courts. In other words, it was restricted to just the important people, not everyday folks like you and me. The Bible's wisdom literature, by contrast, is addressed to *everyone*, including not just royalty but the common person as well. It applies to royalty all the way down to the most basic social unit, the family, as well as the individual. You'll notice that this is a consistent theme in Scripture. One of the many things that makes the Christian tradition and the good news of Jesus Christ so unique is that there is no barrier to entry; it's not a pay-to-play scheme, it's not just for important people, it's not a club—it's open to anyone. So like our faith in general, there is no one whom this book doesn't apply to.

Let's ask some journalism questions. Who wrote Proverbs, and why? It is attributed to King Solomon. This makes sense because according to 1 Kings, Solomon was known for his wisdom:

> And God gave Solomon wisdom and understanding beyond measure, and breadth of mind like the sand on the seashore, so that Solomon's wisdom surpassed the wisdom of all the people of the east and all the wisdom of Egypt. For he was wiser than all other men . . . and his fame was in all the surrounding nations. He also spoke 3,000 proverbs, and his songs were 1,005. He

spoke of trees, from the cedar that is in Lebanon to the hyssop that grows out of the wall. He spoke also of beasts, and of birds, and of reptiles, and of fish. And people of all nations came to hear the wisdom of Solomon, and from all the kings of the earth, who had heard of his wisdom. (1 Kings 4:29–34)

One thing that I'd like to point out is that Solomon's wisdom didn't *compete with* the wisdom of the time; it didn't offer interesting and unique takes on current affairs. It *surpassed* all the wisdom that was available to anyone, anywhere during that time. The wisdom we're talking about surpassing is the wisdom of the Egyptians, who conceived of and built the pyramids.

Solomon is also credited with the Song of Songs and Ecclesiastes. An old Jewish commentary (*Midrash Rabbah*) suggests that the three books represented the three main stages of Solomon's life: a youth concerned with beauty and sensuality; then a middle-aged man concerned with what's right; and finally, an older man who realizes how much he doesn't know. It's also important to bear in mind that "authorship" didn't necessarily involve sitting down and writing like we think of it. Ancient Israel was an oral culture, so it's probably most accurate to think of this as a collection of the wisdom that you would have heard if you had hung around Solomon for long enough.

How should we read it? There are four main parts to the book: an introduction, a collection of lengthy discourses, a collection of one-liners, and a conclusion. The introduction is 1:1–7, and you could think of it as a preamble of sorts, or an executive summary of what's to come. Psalms 1–2 functions in the same way for the following 148 chapters. Proverbs 1–9 consists mostly of practical moral encouragement in the form of several discourses, such as avoiding evil associations, not resisting or avoiding wisdom, the benefits of wisdom, trusting in God, staying on the right path, guarding your heart, avoiding adultery, and some practical warnings against bad loans, laziness, lying, and so on.

Things change with chapter 10 and continue through chapter 22. We get a lot of one-liners, and the themes broaden. Most but not all concern personal conduct and personal relationships. The end of the book is 22:17–31:31. This is a mixture of both one-liners and larger units of material. Most but not all concern public conduct and public relationships. Proverbs 31:10 to the end is the conclusion, and it includes a famous passage describing the characteristics of an "excellent wife." The Hebrew term here is *eshet-chayil* (אֵשֶׁת־חַיִל), with *chayil* actually being the same word that is translated as "mighty" or "valiant," as in a mighty warrior. So we might translate this more literally as "woman of valor." Also, *eshet* can mean "wife" but doesn't necessarily have to; it can simply mean "woman." Thus other translations have this as a "woman of noble character." This is the same term used to refer to Ruth. This chapter has no parallel in ancient Near Eastern literature; there is nothing like it anywhere else.

We know that a central theme of proverbs is *wisdom*. We tend to think of wisdom in didactic terms, that is, teaching, instruction, and advice. That's not wrong, but that's not all there is to it. The Hebrew word for "wisdom" is *hochma* (חָכְמָה). It can mean "teaching, instruction, or advice," but it is also used to refer to wisdom as a *divine attribute*, a principle that is part of God's very life, *the very power of God to create and give life itself.* Listen carefully to how wisdom is portrayed in Proverbs 8:12, 22–31, in the first person:

> I, wisdom, dwell with prudence,
>> and I find knowledge and discretion. . . .
>
> The LORD possessed me at
>> the beginning of his work,
>> the first of his acts of old.
>
> Ages ago I was set up,
>> at the first, before the beginning of the
>> earth.
>
> When there were no depths I was brought forth,
>> when there were no springs abounding
>> with water. . . .
>
> When he established the heavens, I was there . . .
> when he assigned to the sea its limit,
>> so that the waters might not transgress his
>> command,
>
> when he marked out the foundations of the earth,
> then I was beside him, like a master workman,
>> and I was daily his delight,
>> rejoicing before him always,
> rejoicing in his inhabited world
>> and delighting in the children of man.

Wisdom, in other words, is not just practical instruction but the very power of God itself that was present at the foundation of the world. I mentioned earlier how curious it was that the account of Solomon's wisdom in 1 Kings included his knowledge of various creatures. I have a hunch that this is why the writer of 1 Kings specifically included Solomon's knowledge of the created order in the description of why Solomon's wisdom surpassed all other wisdom: Solomon made the connection that we're making now, that wisdom is tied to creation itself.

And when we peel back *that* layer—when we are talking about God's wisdom, word, and power that was present at the beginning of creation itself—that sounds a lot like the opening lines of John's Gospel: "In the beginning was the Word, and the Word was with God, and the Word was God. He was in the beginning with God. All things were made through him, and without him was not any thing made that was made. In him was life, and the life was the light of men. The light shines in the darkness, and the darkness has not overcome it." In other words, that sounds a lot like Jesus. Jesus certainly made use of the wisdom tradition in his ministry. Jesus used proverbs in his teaching. As a matter of fact, the Hebrew word that is translated as "proverb," *mashal* (מָשָׁל), can also be translated as "parable"—and Jesus loved parables. Listen to a few examples of how wisdom shows up in Jesus' ministry:

> And the child grew and became strong, filled with wisdom. And the favor of God was upon him. Now his parents went to Jerusalem every year at the Feast of the Passover. And when he was twelve years old, they went up according to custom. And when the feast was ended, as they were returning, the boy Jesus stayed behind in Jerusalem. His parents did not know it, but supposing him to be in the group they went a day's journey, but then they began to search for him among their relatives and acquaintances, and when they did not find him, they returned to Jerusalem, searching for him. After three days they found him in the temple, sitting among the teachers, listening to them and asking them questions. And all who heard him were amazed at his understanding and his answers. (Luke 2:40–47)

> He went away from there and came to his hometown, and his disciples followed him. And on the Sabbath he began to teach in the synagogue,

and many who heard him were astonished, saying, "Where did this man get these things? What is the wisdom given to him? How are such mighty works done by his hands?" (Mark 6:1–2)

When the crowds were increasing, he began to say, "This generation is an evil generation. . . . The queen of the South will rise up at the judgment with the men of this generation and condemn them, for she came from the ends of the earth to hear the wisdom of Solomon, and behold, something greater than Solomon is here." (Luke 11:29–31)

So Jesus acquired wisdom in his youth, he taught wisdom in a way that caught people off guard, and now there is this insane claim that his wisdom surpasses the wisdom of Solomon . . . which surpassed all the wisdom in the world! Paul escalates things even more. Listen to what he says in 1 Corinthians 1 and Colossians 2:

I want you to know how great a struggle I have for you and for those at Laodicea and for all who have not seen me face to face, that their hearts may be encouraged, being knit together in love, to reach all the riches of full assurance of understanding and the knowledge of God's mystery, which is Christ, *in whom are hidden all the treasures of wisdom and knowledge.* (Col. 2:1–3)

Where is the one who is wise? Where is the scribe? Where is the debater of this age? Has not God made foolish the wisdom of the world? For since, in the wisdom of God, the world did not know God through wisdom, it pleased God through the folly of what we preach to save those who believe. For Jews demand signs and Greeks seek wisdom, but we preach Christ crucified, a stumbling block to Jews and folly to Gentiles, but to those who are called, both Jews and Greeks, Christ the power of God and the wisdom of God. . . . Because of him you are in Christ Jesus, who became to us wisdom from God, righteousness and sanctification and redemption. (1 Cor. 1:20–30)

Jesus Christ was a wise man, but he was so much more than that. He was the embodiment, the incarnation, of the creative, powerful wisdom and Word of God that created and gave life to the world itself. And as we grow in our knowledge of Jesus, we grow in our knowledge of God's powerful, creative wisdom and Word. Now at this point I would normally summarize what we've been discussing and send you on your way with two or three neat and tidy practical suggestions. But the irony here is that Proverbs works the opposite way. It *is* practical. It's the most practical book of Scripture there is.

But because it's so practical, it can be easy to miss the bigger theological connections available beyond just the nuts and bolts of wise living. So let me leave you with a thought about how Proverbs can connect to your faith, no matter who you are (and remember it's addressed to everyone). Most people learn things best by *doing*, not just listening and thinking. If you want to learn how to do something, at some point you've got to close YouTube and get out there and make some mistakes. Likewise, as we heed the practical wisdom of Proverbs in our everyday lives—money, relationships, speech—what I want to suggest to you is that we have an opportunity to do much more than just make good, wise choices. We have the opportunity to learn about the very character of God himself through real-world, hands-on experience.

This is how Christ himself went about things. Eugene Peterson writes: "The ways Jesus goes about loving and saving the world are personal: nothing disembodied, nothing abstract, nothing impersonal. Incarnate, flesh and blood, relational, particular, local. The ways employed in our North American culture are conspicuously impersonal: programs, organizations, techniques, general guidelines, information detached from place."[1] We have the opportunity to grow in our love of Christ by heeding the words of Proverbs, not by abstract, intimidating theological concepts, but by *doing*. And as we learn by doing, as we start walking in wise ways, because wisdom has been with God from the beginning as God's powerful, creative word, we will find that we actually participate in the life of God itself and find our salvation.

1. Eugene Peterson, *The Jesus Way: A Conversation on the Ways That Jesus Is the Way* (Grand Rapids: Eerdmans, 2011), 1.

8

THE NATURE OF SIN

Mark 2:1–12

Over the last several weeks we have been talking about some of the vices that we might encounter in our efforts to follow Christ. Specifically, we've discussed things like consumption, sex, and speech, and some of the ways these things can be used and abused when they're not given their proper place in a well-formed Christian life. What we've been talking about is *sin*, although we haven't been using that term specifically. I am well aware that no one likes this term, and it has a lot of baggage associated with it. Let me reassure you that you're not about to get a lecture about personal behavior and what you should and shouldn't be doing with your spare time. But I do want to explore the topic of sin in more depth because this is one of those things that is foundational to what makes the Christian faith what it is.

Let me start us off with a general definition, and then we'll look at a specific passage from the Gospel of Mark. We often think of sin in terms of individual rights and wrongs, such as the things we discussed over the last few weeks: consumption, sex, and language. That's not wrong, but what I want to suggest to you this morning is *that's not all there is to it*. In fact, the individual acts we typically associate with the word "sin" are really just the tip of the iceberg; they are symptoms of a much more complex disease. The term that Scripture uses to refer to sin most frequently really just means something like "missing the mark." You might think of archery or target shooting. When I miss a target, I don't necessarily intend to do it—it's just that my aim wasn't true or my sight was misaligned. In our personal lives, we don't wake up every day and think, *You know what? Today I'm going to do as many dumb things as I possibly can.* Rather we just have a tendency to do dumb things. Our aim is off. Also, this disease is not limited to human beings; there is a sense in which it applies to the whole created order. The general definition I'd like to suggest this morning is this: *Sin is a general condition of separation from God that affects human beings primarily but also creation itself.* It applies to human beings especially, but the whole created order is in a temporary state of separation from God.

Now let's take a look at a passage from the second chapter of Mark's Gospel.

> And when he returned to Capernaum after some days, it was reported that he was at home. And many were gathered together, so that there was no more room, not even at the door. And he was preaching the word to them. And they came, bringing to him a paralytic carried by four men. And when they could not get near him because of the crowd, they removed the roof above him, and when they had made an opening, they let down the bed on which the paralytic lay. And when Jesus saw their faith, he said to the paralytic, "Son, your sins are forgiven." Now some of the scribes were sitting there, questioning in their hearts, "Why does this man speak like that? He is blaspheming! Who can forgive sins but God alone?" And immediately Jesus, perceiving in his spirit that they thus questioned within themselves, said to them, "Why do you question

these things in your hearts? Which is easier, to say to the paralytic, 'Your sins are forgiven,' or to say, 'Rise, take up your bed and walk'? But that you may know that the Son of Man has authority on earth to forgive sins"—he said to the paralytic— "I say to you, rise, pick up your bed, and go home." And he rose and immediately picked up his bed and went out before them all, so that they were all amazed and glorified God, saying, "We never saw anything like this!" (vv. 1–12)

We obviously would have expected Jesus to first say, "Son, get up and walk" or something similar. Jesus has developed a reputation for physical healing after all, and that's one of the reasons the crowd was there. But I want to suggest that one of the things that we learn from this passage is that in the mind of Jesus, *the spiritual problem of sinfulness was a more urgent problem to address than the physical problem of paralysis.* I also want to suggest that *the spiritual problem of sinfulness and the physical problem of paralysis could be more closely linked* than we sophisticated modern Westerners might like to think.

In the ancient world, mind, body, and soul were a package deal. I don't know about you, but that's how

I'm wired too. When I come down with a fever, it's not just an issue of the body: my mind gets foggy, I can't think straight, I'm unhappy, and so on. It hasn't been until the last couple hundred years that we started thinking in terms of the difference between mind and body. In the Jewish mind of Jesus' day, there was actually a close connection between spiritual sinfulness and physical sickness, not in a causative sense but rather as symptoms of the same disease. In fact the Bablylonian Talmud (*b. Ned.* 41a) suggests, "A sick man does not recover from his sickness until all his sins are forgiven." Sickness can also serve to illustrate the problem of sin, which is a more basic human problem than disease (cf. James 5:15–16; Ps. 103:3; Isa. 38:17). Augustine said something very similar: he emphasized that in the same way that the man in the story is paralyzed physically, we are inwardly paralyzed spiritually. The problem is that our inward paralysis isn't as visible or urgent as outward disease.

Now, Jesus does go on to heal the man's paralysis also. I'd like to make a couple of points here. First, bear in mind that healing in Jesus' ministry always has a *purpose*. It is often used to make a bigger theological point of some sort. In this case, the main point seems to be that Jesus needed to demonstrate his authority to the religious leaders. This was common in the ancient world; physical healings were often used to verify or ratify a teacher's legitimacy. Again, recall how far removed we are culturally from the world of the Bible. Physical healings were common, and they are still common today in some parts of the world. In this case, the physical healing seems to be the easy part. And we learn from Jesus himself that the point of healing in this passage is "so that you may know that the Son of Man has authority on earth to forgive sins." The physical healing is derivative of the bigger spiritual problem. This indicates to me that the real priority in the mind of Jesus is the spiritual disease.

Let me shift gears now and suggest to you that what happens in this story is a snapshot of what is available to all of us. In the first chapter of Ephesians, Paul says—note carefully how excessive Paul's language is—"In [Christ] we have redemption through his blood, the forgiveness of our trespasses, according to the riches of his grace, which he lavished upon us, in all wisdom and insight making known to us the mystery of his will, according to his purpose, which he set forth in Christ as a plan for the fullness of time, to unite all things in him, things in heaven and things on earth."

We can't understand forgiveness if we don't understand the offense. And the offense is not just the little nitpicky things in our private lives that we often obsess over—the offense is much bigger. Our problem isn't necessarily that we do what we shouldn't and don't do what we should, but that we desire to do those things we shouldn't in the first place, and don't always desire the things that we should. We have a tendency to miss the target, and it's not always intentional.

All of creation is infected by separation from God, but here's the key: *God doesn't want it to be this way.* The reason this is important to grasp is that it helps us understand why the death and resurrection of Christ were necessary. The death and resurrection of Jesus wasn't a random event; it was a *solution to a problem.* And if we don't understand the problem that Jesus is the solution to, Jesus' death and resurrection won't make much sense.

This is one of the main reasons why there is so much confusion about the Christian faith in our current cultural moment. The sorts of things we hear from advertising, entertainment, and self-help gurus are things like, "You are so amazing!" "You are perfect!" "You are so awesome!" Now, we can be amazing and beautiful and all those things, but we have to keep in mind that at the same time, we have a huge problem as humans—we are in a state of separation from God. Both things are true: we as human beings were made in the image of God, but in very short order, we managed to make a huge mess of something that God intended to be good.

Some of you are familiar with C. S. Lewis. In his book *Mere Christianity*, Lewis puts it this way: "Christianity tells people to repent and promises them forgiveness. It therefore has nothing (as far as I know) to say to people who do not know they have done anything to repent of and who do not feel that they need any forgiveness."[1] He also suggests in this work that two things are universally true: there is a natural moral law, and we are not very good at following it. He goes on to say very honestly that until

1. C. S. Lewis, *Mere Christianity* (New York: HarperCollins, 1952), 31.

you have accepted the fact that we as human beings are fundamentally imperfect apart from God, the Christian faith just isn't going to make a whole lot of sense. As Paul states, "The word of the cross is folly to those who are perishing, but to us who are being saved, it is the power of God" (1 Cor. 1:18).

Cornelius Plantinga is the former president of one of the schools I attended, and he wrote a well-known book on sin. Pay close attention to the title: *Not the Way It's Supposed to Be*. What he emphasizes in this book is that we are imperfect creatures born into an imperfect world through no choice of our own. But it was not God's original plan for it to be this way, and God has been at work ever since the first chapters of Genesis getting things back on track and healing the world of its self-imposed separation from him. Sin is a general disease that we are all infected with.

I'm running the risk of sounding negative. Please don't let that be your takeaway from this. The whole point of the gospel of Jesus Christ is that it is good news for us. But in order to understand and fully appreciate how good the news of Jesus' victory over death, disease, and suffering is, we've got to first understand what the problem is. *We have to understand the extent of the problem in order to understand the significance of the solution.*

One of the things I love about the story from Mark is that the paralytic and his friends knew there was a problem, they knew exactly how it could be solved, and they did whatever they had to do to get as close to Jesus as they possibly could. I think that's a good lesson for us. The problem is not just me wrestling with my own personal behavior but rather a general condition of death and decay and distortion that applies to all of creation and shows up in all kinds of ways that we are all too familiar with. Feelings of jealousy, envy, hatred? *Not the way it's supposed to be.* Infidelity, abuse, neglect? *Not the way it's supposed to be.* Natural disasters? *Not the way it's supposed to be.* Global health crises? *Not the way it's supposed to be.* The last fifteen months in general? *Not the way it's supposed to be.*

But of course there is good news. God has taken the first step toward us in Jesus Christ and says, "It's okay." If you recognize that all is not well with the world around you and within you, you are off to a good start. And with that in mind, I'd like to close with a paraphrase of the beginning of one of my favorite ancient catechisms. Notice how closely related the problem of sin and the solution in Christ really are:

> My only comfort in life and in death, is that I am not my own, but belong—body and soul, in life and in death—to my faithful Savior, Jesus Christ. He has fully paid for all my sins with his precious blood, and has set me free from the tyranny of evil. He also watches over me in such a way that . . . all things must work together for my salvation. Because I belong to him, Christ, by his Holy Spirit, assures me of eternal life and makes me wholeheartedly willing and ready from now on to live for him.[2]

2. *Heidelberg Catechism*, 450th anniv. ed. (Grand Rapids: Faith Alive, 2013), 8.

Addresses

9

FOLLOWING CHRIST IN
TIMES OF TRANSITION

As of this last Sunday, we have now entered the season of Pentecost. At Christmas we celebrated the birth of Christ among us; during Lent we journeyed with Christ to the cross; at Easter we celebrated his resurrection from the dead; and now we are celebrating God's gift to us in the coming of the Holy Spirit to live within us and among us. This year in particular I want to suggest to you that our church has a unique opportunity to reflect on and celebrate the reassurance, confidence, comfort, and guidance that the Spirit provides to us.

Here's what I mean by this. Our community is right in the middle of some major transitions. It's important to acknowledge this. Almost overnight, we weren't able to meet together in person anymore, and if you've been around our church for long, you know that's a huge part of our life together. Before that, we learned that our pastor and his family were starting a new chapter in their journey. Not long ago, we learned that a new pastor and his family will be coming to join us in July. Before all that, we launched a new campus, and on top of all that, there are still ongoing conversations about the directions our denomination could be headed.

And those are just the major events. Many other things could be mentioned. All things told, this is a unique moment in the life of our church, and quite frankly, it might not seem like the same place that you've grown to know and love. If that's something that has crossed your mind, please hear this: that's okay, our work will go on, and we will continue to pursue our mission.

There's more. As a community of people who follow in the way of Christ, I want to remind you that we are not alone. We are surrounded by what the book of Hebrews calls a "great cloud of witnesses" of imperfect people past and present who have been in our shoes before. God's people have walked through times of transition as we are right now, and in every case, God proved to be faithful. As a matter of fact, God's people are almost always in a transition of some sort, and that's part of what makes the Christian life what it is.

What could this mean for us? I'd like to answer this question at length by offering some brief reflections on moments from Scripture when God's people have been in times of transition and how God worked among them for their benefit. I think these stories can give us as a church confidence, reassurance, and peace as we move forward during our own time of transition into our next chapter as a community who faithfully follows in the way of the resurrected Christ.

Imagine this: you and your spouse are in your mid-seventies, and you have settled down in the town your parents brought you up in. You never had children, which is not necessarily what you wanted, but you've lived a full life, and the sun is setting on your final days.

What comes next? You might recognize these details as the story of Abram and Sarai, later Abraham and Sarah, in Genesis 11–12. This is what things looked like at the end of their lives, but things took a very unexpected turn. In this moment, God comes to them and says this: "*Go* from your country and your kindred and your father's house to the land I will show you. And I will make of you a great nation, and I will bless you and make your name great, so that you will be a blessing" (Gen. 12:1–2).

I don't know about you, but this is not what I would have expected. Abram and Sarai are perfectly fine where they are, but God tells them to get up and go. And not just that, but get up and go, and God won't even tell them where they are going. To make things more interesting, they are to get up and go without knowing where they're going, *and* after all this time of childlessness, God is not only going to grant them children but is going to use their family to bless and benefit the entire world.

That's a lot to take in, but I want to mention a few things in particular. First of all, this is not an outlier story in the biblical narrative; it's at the center of it. It is impossible to overestimate the importance of Abraham and Sarah in the big story of Scripture. In fact, you can draw a straight line from the promise

God makes to Abraham and Sarah here and the life, death, and resurrection of Jesus Christ. Isn't it interesting, then, that such an important moment would not be one of, say, triumph and victory but of uncertainty and trust? At one of the most crucial moments in the entire narrative of Scripture, we find a time of transition that God uses to accomplish his purposes.

Fast-forward toward the end of Scripture in Galatians 3, where the apostle Paul actually goes so far as to say that in this exact moment in Abraham's life, *the gospel was preached to Abraham ahead of time* (Gal. 3:8). He refers to Abraham as "the man of faith"; likewise, the author of the book of Hebrews uses Abraham as an example of faithfulness and hope when he says that Abraham looked forward to what God would do, and Sarah welcomed children into their family because she had confidence in God's ability to do so.

I hope the reassurance for us in our own time of transition is clear. Times of transition are not exceptions on the journey of following in the way of Christ. In fact, transition and uncertainty are built into the very foundation of our faith, and I think that's a good thing. It gives us an opportunity to place our trust and confidence not in ourselves but in God's good work in the world that he loves. I hope you'll continue to join me in not shying away from this time of transition but rather, like Abraham and Sarah, looking forward to what the Spirit of God can do among us as we place our confidence in the resurrected Christ during this season of change.

I mentioned that God promised to bless Abraham and Sarah's family and the whole world through them, so that's what should happen next, right? We would expect things to become increasingly positive. As the story continues, however, we actually find that there's even more transition. Look ahead with me to the next book in Scripture, the book of Exodus, which picks up right where the book of Genesis leaves off: with the descendants of Abraham, the Israelites, in Egypt of all places.

There we learn that things didn't become increasingly positive but that the opposite is the case: we actually read that the Egyptians "ruthlessly made the people of Israel work as slaves and made their lives bitter with hard service, in mortar and brick, and in all kinds of work in the field. In all their work they ruthlessly made them work as slaves" (Exod. 1:13–14). The last we heard, God's promise to Abraham was nothing but blessing, and this is how things turn out? The opposite of what was promised? What is going on?

Listen carefully to what happens next: "The people of Israel groaned because of their slavery and cried out for help. Their cry for rescue from slavery came up to God. And God heard their groaning, and God remembered his covenant with Abraham, with Isaac, and with Jacob. God saw the people of Israel—and God knew." God heard . . . and God remembered . . . and God knew. And what happens after *that* is a story we all know very well: God appears to Moses and calls him to lead his people out of Egypt into the promised land. As a matter of fact, God's last words to Moses right before they make the journey across the Red Sea are these: "Why are you crying out to me? Tell the people to *move forward*" (Exod. 14:15; emphasis added).

Another absolutely crucial defining moment in the biblical story—God revealing himself and speaking audibly to Moses, and rescuing his people from slavery in Egypt—like the story of Abraham and Sarah, is another story of transition, of God taking his people from one place to the next. In both cases, the pattern is the same: God's people are in one situation, but God has grander plans for his people and the world around them.

I think the pattern is not just similar but exactly the same for us as a church: we have grown accustomed to certain ways of doing things, but there are different purposes not just for us but, perhaps more important, for the world around us. As we continue to travel the well-worn path of Pentecost, things will continue to look a little different around our church for a while, but we have every reason to trust in the good work that God has started here. And we have every reason to look forward in hope in our own time of transition. We are in good company.

Now, there actually was an extended period of time in the Old Testament during which God's people were *not* in transition. In fact, they settled, got comfortable, and built a kingdom. And *this*, not the times of transition, is where things begin to take a turn for the worse. Some time after Israel leaves Egypt after the exodus, they decide they're tired of following in God's ways. At one point they actually complain that it would have been better to have stayed in slavery in Egypt rather than deal with the uncertainty that comes with following in God's way. So what do they do? In 1 Samuel 8, we learn that the people of Israel demand to have a king like all the other nations around them.

This is a tragic moment in the ongoing story of Scripture in my opinion, and after this moment, things do not go well. Throughout the remainder of the two books of Samuel and the two books of Kings, and as retold in the two books of Chronicles, generation after generation after generation forgets and neglects God and his ways, and God gradually recedes into the background of the story.

There's an interesting admonition for us as a church here. Our own period of transition continues. We're between pastors, we'll continue to see some different faces preaching at both campuses over the next few weeks, and our seating arrangements and hospitality look different. We might not be crazy about all this. But consider the alternative, and consider the lesson from the history of Israel: the real problems begin to creep in when God's people start to get comfortable, not during times of transition and uncertainty.

The alternative—getting settled and doing things our own way—can lead to forgetfulness and neglect, but moving forward in humility and faith, one step at a time, is a well-worn and trustworthy path in the Christian journey.

Thankfully, we know this isn't how things end. We learn from the Gospels that even when God's people turn their backs on him, God doesn't walk away but actually comes to us in Jesus Christ. The pages of the New Testament teach us that the events we have explored the past few weeks are finally embodied and summarized in Jesus. If that's the case, we might expect to see something like the establishment of a new kingdom, or maybe the construction of a massive new building in Jerusalem to commemorate the occasion, or maybe a massive festival of some sort. But let's remember our roots. God often works in ways we don't expect, and the same is true of the life and work of Jesus Christ. He does announce a kingdom, but it's one that flies under the radar; he does commemorate the occasion in Jerusalem, but through his death and resurrection, not by constructing a monument or a memorial; and he does throw feasts, but not with the people he's supposed to associate with.

And one of the things you'll notice about Jesus' work is that he's always on the move. He never stays in one place for very long. When he recruits his disciples, he doesn't say, "Here's your job, and you do this," but rather "Come, follow me." When they ask him who the greatest, most influential figures are in his kingdom, he points to the children and teaches us to be humble. When Jesus is transfigured before Peter and James, they say to him, "Lord, let's set up camp and stay here," but Jesus says to them, "Get up, don't be afraid, let's go."

Once again we see that in the life of faith, there is something central and important about transition and uncertainty. Even Jesus himself, the author and perfecter of our faith, never established anything in the way we might expect a dignitary to, but rather he lived a life of itinerant service and dependence on God. A famous passage from Philippians 2 teaches us that "being found in human form, he humbled himself by becoming obedient to the point of death, even death on a cross. Therefore God has highly exalted him and bestowed on him the name that is above every name" (vv. 8–9). Paul also says at the beginning of this passage that we are to be likeminded. We too are to be humble and hopeful. We too are not to lose hope, but rather to get up, fear not, and get going. We have every reason to be confident in the work that the Spirit of God can do among us—not in spite of our own time of transition but because of it.

The book of Acts picks up where the Gospels leave off, and it continues the story of what happened after Christ's ascension. Chapter after chapter in the book of Acts, we read about how the earliest Christians not only survived but grew and thrived during a time when they were misunderstood, imprisoned, and on the move. Initially, the earliest Christians are in Jerusalem, where they receive the gift of the Holy Spirit at Pentecost. But once again, we see a familiar pattern: God's people don't stay put but rather journey out from Jerusalem and plant seeds of the gospel all around the region. The unexpected promise that God made to Abraham back in Genesis 12 is finally being fulfilled, and all are welcome into God's kingdom.

The book of Acts also introduces us to the apostle Paul, who makes a radical and unexpected transition from being an enemy of the faith to its most outspoken advocate and the author of much of the New

Testament. Like some of the other characters we've been considering over the last few weeks, Paul is not called to settle down and get comfortable in his ways. To the contrary, we learn that he meets resistance and is occasionally beaten and imprisoned for his teaching. I don't know about you, but I wouldn't have expected the fulfillment of God's promise to Abraham to look like a prison cell or a falsely accused criminal on a cross.

But remember that God doesn't always work in ways that we expect. And one of the things I'd like to emphasize from Paul's experience is that when things don't go as planned—when God's promises are fulfilled through what by all measures appears to be failure and imprisonment—Paul doesn't complain or quit or pray for God to change his circumstances. At the end of Acts 4, Paul prays instead for God to simply give him the courage to stay the course. And that's all it takes.

We are not facing anything like what Paul and the earliest Christians faced. However, I do think we can learn from Paul during our own time of ongoing transition. First, we continue to see that God's most important work is often done in times of change.

Second, we can learn from Paul's example in choosing how we respond to uncertainty. Paul would have been well within his rights to decide things were becoming too strange, and just go in another direction. Instead, we learn that Paul prayed for courage to stay the course. I think the encouragement for us is clear: let us pray for courage and confidence to stay the course in our season of uncertainty as we continue to focus on our mission.

I want to briefly conclude by reiterating a couple of terms I have referred to several times: "walking" and "journeying." One thing we learn from the book of Acts is that one of the names that was given to the earliest Christians was "followers of the Way." I like this term because it reminds us that our faith in Christ is not something that we achieve once and for all, and then stop and rest upon arrival. Rather it's an ongoing journey, full of ups and downs, twists and turns. It will always be that way as long as we walk the earth.

This was true for Abraham and Sarah, Moses and the Israelites in the exodus from Egypt, Jesus himself, the apostle Paul, and so many more major figures from our past. God's people specialize in times of transition and in looking forward in hope. Recall that the last thing Moses heard from God before one of the most intimidating moments in the life of Israel—the crossing of the Red Sea—was this: "Why are you crying out to me? Tell the people to move forward" (Exod. 14:15). That is my encouragement for us as we continue to navigate an uncertain season together and walk the road of Pentecost and beyond. Like the Israelites leaving Egypt, let us move forward in joining God's good work around us in the world that he loves.

10

BIBLICAL THEOLOGY AND THE CHRISTIAN LIFE

We have been exploring one of the most challenging topics there is in this class: God. There are lots of different ways to speak about God. That is what the word "theology" literally means—"speaking about God." We have discussed biblical theology, and that means a few different things. It means speaking about God in a way that is biblical, or using Scripture as our guide for speaking about who God is and what God is like. It can also mean allowing Scripture to discipline and regulate our speech about God. But biblical theology also entails a certain understanding of what Scripture is—Scripture is not just a collection of random inspirational sayings or nuggets of wisdom, although it does contain these things. Biblical theology teaches us that Scripture is one unified story, complete with a beginning, middle, and end. Christians often refer to this unified story as having three or four parts: creation, fall, and redemption; or creation, fall, redemption, and new creation.

We also talked about the Christian life. In the same way that we discussed what Scripture is not—that is, it is not just a collection of inspirational sayings—we can also say what the Christian life is not: it is not just a collection of inspirational *moments*, a life broken up into periods of time here and there when Christianity might happen to be interesting or convenient. It's also not a life that's neatly divided up into Christian and non-Christian activities. It's an entire life from start to finish dedicated to knowing and following Christ.

I suggested that the best, most reliable, and most trustworthy place to start in developing a Christian worldview is with who God is and what God is like. That's where the unique Christian belief that God is *triune* is significant. God is not primarily an angry judge, for instance, but first and foremost a loving Father. God exercises judgment, yes, but only in the same way that a loving father disciplines his child—that is, out of love and in his child's best interest. When we read the biblical account of creation in light of this, creation takes on a different and more excellent meaning: God saw that it was *very good*. God does not create out of a need to complete a deficiency but rather out of the overflow of his eternal love. Michael Reeves has this to say: "What makes Christianity absolutely distinct is the identity of our God. *Which* God we worship: *that* is the article of faith that stands before all others."[1]

But we humans managed to mess things up. Here's how we described the problem in this class. We were created by God's love to be participants in God's eternal life of love, but we turned that love inward toward ourselves. Augustine and Martin Luther refer to this as *cor incurvatus in se*—the heart is turned in on itself. This is what sin is—not just individual moral choices we might or might not make any given day, but a state of separation, misdirection, and estrangement from God, the giver of life itself. Scripture teaches us in Romans 8 that the entire creation now suffers from our estrangement from God. "The creation

1. Michael Reeves, *Delighting in the Trinity: An Introduction to the Christian Faith* (Downers Grove, IL: InterVarsity Press, 2012), 16.

waits with eager longing," it tells us. "Sin" is both plural and singular: it is both particular choices that individual people make *and* a general condition that applies to all of creation.

This is an enormous problem, and somehow, Jesus Christ is God's solution to it. But remember that because we believe that God is triune, it is somehow God himself who is present in Christ. Christ wasn't sent by some distant, uninvolved God to complete a transaction. It is God himself who subjects himself to the evil we have created in order to transform it, redeem it from the inside out.

The good news doesn't stop there. God is also Spirit—*pneuma* (πνεῦμα), meaning "breath, wind, spirit, soul." He is the ever-present giver of new life in the midst of a broken, imperfect, and estranged—in other words, sinful—creation. And God gives that Spirit to us. By the Spirit, we can be reoriented back toward God and others as it was in the beginning. Father, Son, and Spirit: one God forever and ever.

How different this God is from the "default" gods of our age, particularly certain forms of deism, or the general, nonspecific belief in a distant god somewhere who might occasionally be involved in the world when we need him to be. Christian Smith calls this approach to faith "Moralistic Therapeutic Deism"—the belief in a god in general who wants us to be nice and happy and is available to help us solve our problems. No holiness, no glory, no sin to make things complicated and judgmental, no sanctification, no Eucharist, no church . . . no Trinity. "This God is not Trinitarian," Smith states. "This God is not demanding. He actually can't be, since his job is to solve our problems and make people feel good."[2]

No, in the beginning God created . . . and it was good . . . and God never stopped being involved. In fact, we could even say that God has a mission for creation. Reeves taught us about who the Triune God is and why that is important for our understanding of God; but we can't stop there. We are also called to cooperate with what the Triune God is doing in his good world: to participate by God's grace in the

2. Christian Smith, *Soul Searching* (New York: Oxford University Press, 2009), 165.

work God is doing through the Spirit—not because we must, but because we may.

So how did God go about achieving his great purpose in creation, and how do we cooperate in it? Here's a hint: *the gospel begins in Genesis*. First of all, the Lord said to Abram, "Go . . . I will make of you a great nation . . . and in you all the families of the earth with be blessed." Note the promise of blessing comes first in response to the problem of sin, then the deliverance from Egypt—salvation in every conceivable respect—and then the giving of the "rules" that we tend to associate with the Old Testament. If you don't learn anything else from this course, learn this: first, God saves.

We follow a God who first saves, and who then asks us to do righteousness and justice—that is, making things right, fixing what is wrong—in response, not because we *have* to but because we are *invited* to. Both testaments refer to God's people as a kingdom of priests—that is, mediators—and a holy nation— that is, a group of people who are set apart for service, people who are called out of darkness into light, and who are a light for the world. In other words, we are witnesses, a word that we often use as a verb but in Scripture is used as a noun. We *are* witnesses to what God has done so that we can *be* witnesses in the world for the world's benefit, and God sends us out into the world—into the public square, into the earthly city—to verify who he is.

We are part of a big story, and the Triune God is the primary character. Creation is the setting, and we as members of Christ's church are important but ultimately supporting characters. When Christ taught us to pray, he taught us not to pray for ourselves—the words "I," "my," or "me" aren't mentioned once in the Lord's Prayer—but for God's will to be done on the earth. Toward that end, we can play any number of roles—engineers, businesspeople, ministers, nurses, athletes, teachers, pilots. Both the specific occupation and the specific ways in which we go about it matter. Our occupations have both instrumental and intrinsic value. Are we benefiting God's world with our time and talents—in other words, are we participating in God's mission for creation—or are we doing something else?

I hope this class has given you a good foundation to go and do whatever it is you think you want to do in God's world, to remember your place in God's ongoing history, and to be a blessing in deep, meaningful, and lasting ways "to the end of the earth." I thank God for you all, wish you well, and offer this prayer as you go on your way:

> The LORD bless you and keep you;
> the LORD make his face to shine upon you and
>   be gracious to you;
> the LORD lift up his countenance upon you and
>   give you peace. (Num. 6:24–26)

AFTERWORD

Many years ago I helped publish a small volume of English translations of two sermons by Karl Barth.[1] The first sermon, delivered in Safenwil early in Barth's career, was given on the occasion of the sinking of the Titanic. The young Barth made a point to address this tragedy in his sermon. The second, delivered more than twenty years later in Bremen, was given during the height of World War II and Adolf Hitler's rule. Ironically, Barth makes no mention whatsoever of Hitler, the war, or anything of the sort in the second sermon. "The difference between the two sermons is clear," Eberhard Busch states in his foreword. "In the first text the newspaper report leads the thought and is then also illuminated by biblical words. In contrast, in the second sermon the Bible text is clearly 'the master' of the thought and so it has

---

1. Karl Barth, *The Word in This World: Two Sermons by Karl Barth*, ed. Kurt Johanson, trans. Christopher Asprey (Vancouver: Regent College Publishing, 2007).

the freedom to illuminate the contemporary events and to orient them in the world."[2]

The majority of the sermons in this volume were given between 2019 and 2021, a time of great uncertainty, anger, and suspicion on a global scale. Crises come and go, however, and I have learned from Barth that sometimes the best way to deal with them theologically, ironically, is to simply ignore them and trust in God's providence. Not always, but sometimes. As William Willimon states in the same volume, "It is as if the preacher, in true service to the congregation, is driven to the text . . . that stands above our context, the text that speaks a word that we, in our fearful situation, could never speak to ourselves."[3] It is my belief that "fearful situations" in any time provide us with opportunities to understand the Word of God in uncommonly clear ways, particularly since "God gave us a spirit not of fear but of power and love and self-control" (2 Tim. 1:7). May we always have the ears to hear.

2. Eberhard Busch, foreword to Barth, *Word in This World*, 9.

3. William Willimon, introduction to Barth, *Word in This World*, 21–22.